Elephants in Love

PATTY SCHOLTEN

Elephants in Love
and other poems

English versions by
JAMES BROCKWAY

London Magazine Editions

First published in Great Britain 2001
by London Magazine Editions
30 Thurloe Place, London SW7 2HQ
Originally published in Dutch
by Atlas, Herengracht 481,1017BT Amsterdam
Copyright © 2001 Patty Scholten
Translation copyright © 2001 James Brockway
ISBN 0-904388-87-5
Set in Monotype Ehrhardt by
Rowland Phototypesetting Ltd
Printed in Great Britain by
St Edmundsbury Press Ltd
both of Bury St Edmunds, Suffolk

A CIP catalogue record for this book
is available from the British Library

The publication of *Elephants in Love*
has been made possible through the financial
support of the Foundation for the
Production and Translation of
Dutch Literature, Amsterdam

Some of these poems first appeared
in *London Magazine*, *Poetry Review*, *The Rialto*
Acumen, *Poetry Wales*, *Lines*, *The Shop*, *The Frogmore Papers*

CONTENTS

INTRODUCTION

Early in May 1999, while making some attempt to follow medical advice and 'take things easy', I received a small book and card from Patty Scholten, a Dutch poet by then known to many, but not to me. The card bore a caricature of poet Simon Vinkenoog, drooping over a daisy. In the 'fifties, Vinkenoog had acted as a sort of choreographer for the young Experimentalist poets, at the time a revolutionary force much like the Angry Young Men in England a few years later. The drawing was by a Belgian author, Hugo Claus, who had made himself the most prominent of all contemporary Belgian writers, as novelist, playwright and everything else. A position he has never since relinquished. With these two as her ushers, Patty Scholten presented me with her new collection of poems, *Traliedieren* (Animals behind Bars), all sonnets, all witty, lively and contemporary in mood, and almost all concerned with animals she had observed in zoos. Would I be interested in translating one, about a shark, wanted for use in an aquarium in New

Orleans? Interested in translating more than one, perhaps?

It did not take long to see this was exactly the sort of work I had been warned to avoid: exacting, requiring concentrated mental effort. These were all fully rhymed sonnets, perfectly rounded and requiring the same formal treatment in English. To arrive at versions in another language which respect the meaning and mood, the rhyme patterns and rhythms of the original, without feeling in the end 'I've spoilt it', is hard work and can leave the translator biting his lip with dissatisfaction and regret he ever started. Better to say 'no', kindly.

One morning I had the letter of refusal ready in my head when I spied an old envelope, with a stub of pencil lying beside it. Taking the book the poet had sent me, I sat down and opened it at the Shark poem and before I knew what I was doing, began translating. That evening the translation was ready for the word processor and the next day despatched. The work had been so entertaining and there was so much about Scholten's manner that appealed to me, that it had gone far more smoothly than I had anticipated. By the time the response arrived, I was already on to the next sonnet and translating this work became an addiction. If I was not busy with it, I felt unwell and unhappy. Besides, I sensed a message here that it was worth working to put across. Apart from Scholten's amusingly original way with words, her dexterity with them, she proved to have a special eye for observing animals. They are observed and described with sympathy and humour but are not sentimentalised or anthropomorphised. They remain animals. They can bite. Her sonnets also amount to an invitation to revise our thinking concerning the relationship between them and ourselves.

Scholten's first collection, *Het Dagjesdier*, appeared in

1995. The word does not exist and is typical of the poet's inventiveness. In Dutch 'Dagjesmens' means 'Day-tripper' and 'dier' means animal. So 'Dagjesdier' is her neologism for an animal in the zoo. The book attracted attention and became a candidate for the big VSB literary prize the next year. Being a nominee for a literary prize in Holland attracts more than ordinary media coverage and a second collection, *Ongekuste Kikkers* (Unkissed Frogs), followed the next year. This collection contained eleven sonnets devoted to people as well as poems on animals, though animals led the way and dominate.

Traliedieren, her third volume, from which I took the sonnets for the translations here, appeared in 1999 and unites the first two collections between the same covers. In the meantime Patty Scholten had shown herself to be an excellent performer of her poetry. According to one report at the annual Night of Poetry in Utrecht 1998, her reading excelled that of poets already noted for their performing prowess. It is not surprising that she began her working life, while still at school, assisting in Artis, the big Amsterdam zoo. Her adroitness in depicting animals in her sonnets will also have something to do with her being trained in her youth at Holland's most famous cartoon studio, Marten Toonder's. She already had a career as a successful deviser of strip cartoon storylines for the young before she emerged as a poet.

In my time I have translated many types of Dutch poetry and I have often found that the work proceeded the more smoothly the bigger the author's reputation. But I had never before experienced the feeling I was working with the original poet in the same room, at the same table, as I enjoyed, translating Patty Scholten's animal sonnets. When actually I was working alone.

Her poems are about animals but they are at the same time about herself, a human being, with something unusual to say, which she does with a sense of fun. And wittily.

JAMES BROCKWAY

Elephants in Love

Here a hellish din is dominant.
I think it's perhaps a gardener trimming trees
with a chain-saw at full blast. But, if you please,
it turns out to be an amorous elephant.

Against her flabby flank his head keeps banging.
She stiffens to resist him in her fashion.
to oppose this bold musician's raging passion.
Or is she only trying to keep standing?

Now they're stood like bookends, head to head,
and lovingly weave and wind their trunks together,
as though two snakes had taken their loving over.
His trunk then measures up her bumps instead.

Those who say: instinct, nothing more or less,
should watch these giant sacks of tenderness.

Baby Elephant

He's very small but already quite a lad,
hemmed in by aunts, fat hens, all unaware,
he gets a push, lands on his derrière,
stands up again – bulldozers aren't that bad.

His ears are flat, like pancakes underdone,
or cauliflower leaves; he stuffs a leek, will rake
and rout about, his trunk a rummy snake,
a divining-rod: from where does water come?

He hops and flaps about a bit, aloof,
follows his trunk, than finds – oh good!
the source of eternal elephantine youth.

His drinking-pool lies hidden to one side
in a mass of grey tree-tunks, a pillared wood
where baby elephants can always hide.

Tapir

He is the blueprint for the elephant,
this tapir with his queer truncated trunk –
to grab him, should he try to do a bunk? –
It sniffs my hand, is pliable but blunt.

A tongue lolls out, a kind of rubber band
with which he plans to lubricate my wrist.
But as for me – I'd rather he'd desist.
It's black with soil and now so is my hand.

Yet there's something to his wettish way to greet.
Another way of labelling, I'd suggest,
of fellow mammals: are they sour or sweet?

Maybe it's the only contact that's worthwhile,
that can ever exist between us, man and beast:
a look, a lick, and then a swap of soil.

Rhino

This rhino on those stumps of legs they've got
slumps down and then rolls over rightaway –
a messy, slapped-down wagonload of clay,
or a clown who's acting 'dead' from dummy shot.

His false nose makes his eyes seem minimal,
turning him into a soulful Cyrano,
or perhaps they're meant to be like that just so
he needn't always look that miserable.

Massive, he now lies basking in the sun
and all he wants to do is twitch his ears,
two funnels for pouring information in.

I wish him showers of sunshine, only tears
of rain, birds to pick out each parasite
and mates who will not judge him by his weight.

Puma on Heat

She sings this canticle: no trumpet's stress
but a hoarse and raucous howl – a thunderstorm.
Startling the visitors with such loud bad form.
She'd move the mountains, this mountain lioness.

She growls like some vociferous vedette,
is unaware this way she'll catch no beau –
he's already there, he shares her bungalow,
and follows (bit deaf) his bruiterous brunette.

Till she settles – muscle wrapped in tawny fur.
He sniffs at, meditates, her glorious rear,
while Daisybelle resumes her aria.

Gently he licks and nibbles at her skin,
as if to say: O.K.? May I come in?
And yes, he may. She'll be a pumama.

Tiger

A demon mask, forged by time and heat.
Jaws open to emit a soundless yawn.
Body erect, taut stripes describe his form.
Fur undulates in rhythm with his gait.

His amber eyes have passed me over, for
behind the wall that keeps us both at bay,
I'm out of reach – to him I'm dummy prey.
He doesn't like me but would eat me raw.

Bored, this killer yawns some more, displays
a rosy cave of pure-white stalactites.
Strolls on again, then crouches, urinates.
I know that cat-like look, that distant gaze.

A dove sweeps high above his cage below.
We're friends again? I ask. The answer's no.

Black Panther

Should his little nephew cross your path, they say,
that means bad luck will soon be taking charge.
But he's bad luck in velvet written large,
when he slinks past, death's never far away.

Languid he lies along a limb – a feat:
all he need do like this is slither off.
His daggers are in their sheaths but quick enough
to kill for the day's essential supply of meat.

Now, for the moment, he's switched his headlamps out
but those little ears are still on full alert
as, patient, he lies asleep: a fat, black cat.

Evil is always black, while good is white.
Black is harmless here. And yet, and yet –
Beware: those jaws, those lily-white teeth – they bite.

Pair of Panthers

They've made a kingdom for them they can keep,
with sand and bars and a big tree overhead.
Reduced to a cat-tray now, their jungle's dead.
Here man's the wolf and they the placid sheep.

The female's rather smaller and more bold.
Her spotted coat's a dress where yesterday,
through leaves the light and shadow used to play.
He bites the gauze above her head. It's cold.

The visitors stand and watch, shyly amused.
They feel themselves imprisoned too, abused
by rules which make them live their lives by halves.

We ruin our teeth as we grind them on the gauze
of society, marriage, bosses, and their laws.
The panthers go to sleep. A wise bird laughs.

Lynx

Don't trust this lady, she's far too smart and pert.
A beauty too – a bearded demoiselle,
swishing that pretty turned-up stump of tail,
paws piously folded, eyes on the alert.

Soft slippers hide claws so sharp it's harrowing.
Ears sprout tufts of hair in grey and black,
that show two thumbprints when she pulls them back.
At times you can see her pupils narrowing.

She's got a cage with rock-and-bush disguise
and iron bars – it's a one-day fly that flies
in there: a chase, a leap, and its story's told.

But here her hunting skills just waste away,
they're redundant now a shop supplies her prey.
Glumly she chews – this cold meat leaves her cold.

Giraffe

The sun lights up the trellis on his coat.
The baby horns, black-tufted, seem too sly
for one who sometimes looks so very shy,
pouting his velvet lips, his thoughts afloat.

How did this swaying temple come to be?
I imagine four legs clutched tight in one tight hand,
his head in the other and tug – it must expand
with a sports-school-trained Creator as M.C.

What can he see up there, what can be spied?
Lions become ginger cats, minute and meek,
the python a mere earthworm at his side.
To wind yourself round him would be pure cheek.

A beast who cannot crawl, nor can he hide.
Yet he can reach the topmost, juiciest leaf.

Zebras

Their coal-black stripes are only caramel –
more brown than black. The pop-art ponies go,
swishing their fly-swats briskly to and fro,
around the savannah-ring they know too well.

They shy and shiver from the fun they're making,
bray as their aimless play of lines assembles.
Here, behind bars, their black and white resembles
a convict's suit to stop them from escaping.

Their mothers they know from the stripes across her hide.
Add one – and her son goes looking everywhere,
searching for her, while she's stood there by his side.

As for me, with bar-code messages I know I'm
illiterate and therefore quite aware
as a zebra, I'd be an orphan-child in no time.

Camels

Nose in the air, lips pursed, head after head,
a train of camels sways across the sand.
One lies still there, a lump of hilly land,
staring at me as though to say: Drop dead.

Nearby, a foal – till ten he's still an ambler.
Well brought-up, he copies mum and dad,
that self-opinionated look they've always had,
his knobbly legs can't take it any longer.

These ships of the desert, these swingers – but I fear
there's something about their humps I can't explain:
sometimes they're stiff and sometimes soft again.

Perhaps that's the reason for those haughty eyes.
A macho, but never sure how high he'll rise,
whether his stand will stand or disappear.

Llama

Sheep's torso raised on stilts, a creamy pelt
round tall white legs, black plaid on back, a bit
manhandled by the heavenly launderette,
now hanging down, all rags. A skin like felt.

His eyes seem rather full of llama care, I'd say.
He eats and spits like a lord, his jaws are huge.
He chews, regurgitates, and chews and chews.
His ears are fingers in a shadow play.

There's a little llama too, but he's half-baked.
His eyes have still their baby-blue-ey glow.
A cuddly toy, white, black, with woolly nap.

But soon the moult will make him grey and streaked
and out of that little Disney snout will grow
a fearsome, yellow pair of shears that snap.

Bisons

Blocks of rock, the bisons at their hay,
mossy, old as their beards, immovable,
their shoulders, massive, sloping towards the tail,
they reach up to their rack, then chew away.

A bunch of short and curlies on their head,
and moony eyes as in a young girl's dream.
Each nostril puffs out its little cloud of steam –
proof that the dying volcano's not yet dead.

Now you think, of course, that here it is my plan
to mourn the slaughter of the buffalo,
its near-extinction at the hand of man.

But for that you must go to others more au fait.
Here I was only out to tell you how
I watched the bisons feed, and breathe, today.

Collared Peccaries

A pack of wild boars covered in black hair,
their long snouts fitted, it seems, with electric plugs,
with highly polished, varnished even, hooves,
turn their back on me (to make me disappear).

The feeble-minded think, of course, like this,
but they're scared inside that tough, brown, brushlike skin.
They dig with their noses – it's sand they're digging in,
with the mad obsession of manic drug addicts.

Four piglets, all with ringlets of white fur,
snuffle and grunt round mummy's belly, where
they know they'll find the milk-bar underneath.

Their desert's like a brilliant, sunlit strand.
Idyllic, but it's pretty gritty, and
you'll find there's always sand between your teeth.

Bears

The fagged-out dancing bears have been set free.
They rush out wildly, stagger, loll and lurch.
Their noses like a dog's, a perfect tool to search
for cosy spots to lie in comfortably.

Although they're still called Mascha, Gert and Jos,
they no longer have to go through all their paces.
Instead they lie asleep and hide their faces,
head between paws, tangled hills of moss.

Such freedom after an unfair prison term
seems just, at very least. The nose-ring gone,
and all around a wood of bright, new chances.

But in their sleep old images return
of who was boss and said what must be done,
and Bruin's afraid and dances, dances, dances.

Baboons

Fatigued, the baboons perch in the failing light,
tired but proud, high on their monkey rock.
Successful mountaineers of sturdy stock –
a Red Indian look-out post on the alert.

Their furry hoods on which the floodlight's shined,
have golden aureoles. The stumpy snout,
devoid of hair and rubbery, juts out,
but discreetly concealed, each red and raw behind.

One sings a soft, nocturnal lullaby –
it's a muted growl, not so melodious
as the rock-high song sung by that Lorelei.

Perhaps in monkey terms he wants to sing:
"We baboons have become mere seconds, not first choice,
now man's thought up that evolution thing."

Orang-Utan

This orang-utan male has grown to know me.
He comes and squats down slyly by the pane
to watch me while I'm here – time and again,
yet still that honest jungle snout can throw me.

I itch to entertain him in his prison,
to give him a spontaneous demonstration.
His eyes grow small, contract with concentration,
when I open up my handbag to his vision.

I show him my notebook, pen, a little comb,
switch on my lighter, keep it twisting, turning,
even lift out my lipstick from its home.

Close bag, get up – empty, my hands are learning.
Now every single thing's been checked and shown,
I flee, feel in my back two dark eyes burning.

Death's Head Monkeys

They sit perched in the trees like little poems,
Nature's lyrics cast in haiku size.
Not skeleton-skulls but lively little eyes,
set in mustard-yellow faces; hooded gnomes.

Snow White's dwarfs, whose every digit delves –
Heigh-ho, Heigh-ho, fast, furry fingers grab
from the public's pocket, shopping-basket, bag.
An athletic club of kleptomanic elves.

They size each visitor up with expert eye.
That child there, with that choc-ice, that's for me.
No scream, no wail, can stop a thief so fleet.

Then, as they go, they nip a kid or two
with lightning little teeth – Boo-hoo! Boo-hoo!
while gibbering blithely: 'Small' does not mean 'sweet'.

Mother Gorilla

Her left hand's hers no more, no more herself,
but holds this heap of ape, her life, her light.
It's demanding, mother love. The counterweight
rests in her arm: her new, black-bearded elf.

Rest's not the word – he's on a different tack.
He flails his arms, his legs, he pricks his ears,
huge discs designed to make quite sure he hears.
She supports his little head. She pats his back.

Close-by a brawny sack of muscles waits.
That's Tarzan, with Lombroso head, the father.
He contemplates his offspring with distaste.

Just once, alas, she let him have his way.
She turns aside and should he stump up further,
She'll know some tricks to keep the beast at bay.

Flamingos

Their bodies a comma, necks a question-mark,
they step so circumspectly through the reeds
as if their pool were filled with shrimps, not weeds.
Their speech a queer toot-tooting, then a bark.

A babel, a throat with many a, many a tongue,
but then staccato, a monotonous note, a drone,
that ends with a leaking bagpipe-moan, a groan
so plaintive, you'd think their necks were being wrung.

Those necks they coil and twist in hairpin bends
to lay along their backs, calm and correct,
like weary snakes with which their pink down blends.

Much ballet, song and dance, yet it regales:
I imagine I'm in an opera by Brecht
with, in the intervals, the Chippendales.

Vulture

In search of corpses, his gimlet eyes peer round,
but day-tripper crowds are not the dying sort.
He races wildly about, as though caught short,
then stops to take me in, dead or unsound.

A hunchback, hunching shoulders in despair,
moth-eaten fur grown scraggy round his neck,
a slimy dribble hanging from curved beak –
an incontinence known to all teetotallers.

Above his cage grey cloud still chases cloud,
but never again will he circle round the void,
his hunting season's been shut down for good.

Tucked away wings are now left unemployed.
Claws are daggers deprived of dagger-food.
Now it is on revenge the fierce eyes brood.

Humming-Bird

In films you always see him with the aid
of slow-motion cameras – in reality
he's like a brightly-painted giant bee,
or simply what he is – a brilliant bird.

It's the mini-surgery of tulip, rose.
Twittering, he flies circles round the bud
in which he knows there's nectar to be had,
then expertly he siphons as he goes.

The humming-bird departs, leaves to migrate.
A rocket fuelled with honey for a flight
of miles and miles of nothing else but air.

His jewelled colours are his own affair.
They're prisms that reflect the sun's fierce light.
Like him, they're already gone before you've sighed.

Oystercatcher

He comes and joins me, seeming quite at ease,
as I scrutinize this concrete North Sea strand,
constructed here by man's almighty hand.
he waddles round me, black and white, then sees

my shoes and at once is taken by the eyes
for the laces – here's some special kind of perk!
This pointed yellow beak now sets to work.
Something delicious here – a real surprise!

His clever eyes, two beads, soon recognize
my laces for what they are: fake, look-like food.
He's not having that, he seeks a richer prize.

Searching with him, I go on digging too
into this look-like beach, but it's no good.
If only I'd stuffed real worms into my shoe.

Alligator

A fearsome blast of air – a tyre, a leak? –
shoots out of his throat, if you make his hackles rise.
The alligator's silent otherwise
between his badly regulated teeth.

Each eye's a curved, pagoda-roofed glass pane,
slime-green; each pupil a thin, a jet-black slit.
His jaw half-open, in which quite soon he'll fit
his frightened prey, who'll fight and thrash in vain.

A mere quiver on the surface. It causes you
at most unease. You don't give it a thought or
stop to think. Perhaps a cough or two.

Death may come like that when it's your time.
That black tree-trunk there, floating in the water:
his barque – of freight and ferryman no sign.

Seals

A black-capped swimmer stares straight up at me,
inspects me with astonished, childlike eyes,
then starts to wave and splash to show surprise.
His name in Dutch is 'Rob' though he's a she.

Her mate lies quietly drying on the strand,
a shiny lump of wet, black liquorice.
Fishbone hairs on his snout make a moustache.
He dives and leaves no single trace behind.

He's in his element here, here he's at home.
Sun and sea to splash about in, brood in.
The water has a silver lid, a dome.

It's made of floor on floor of fish and light.
The flooded cellar's meant for keeping food in.
The attic's meant to practise breathing right.

Sea-Cow

He glides through the water, devoid of sail or fin,
a torpid torpedo from some fairytale.
Too plump for a dolphin, too small to be a whale.
Perhaps a crashed, anaemic zeppelin?

He bobs about a bit, then vegetates,
a phantom, with two nostrils up on top,
no more – too massive, meek, too fast to flop.
A form that fashions the dreams he instigates:

In the eager sailor, reaching out with lust,
who spies in the waves a girl with mermaid's tail
and plunges – to find it's seaweed that he's kissed.

In the poet, who found his inspiration sank
and let the sirens lure him with their wail.
A splash. The ink has run. His paper's blank.

Shark

A perfect rudder, his tail jerks steadily,
his course is set on something edible.
His dorsal fin a flag that warns us all:
a shark swims where he knows his food will be.

In his flashing flesh, five radiator slits,
those are his gills; his eyes look awful queer –
the cockpit windows of a Boeing where,
though out of sight, you know the pilot sits.

I'm here, in the aquarium, where at twelve o'clock
you can watch the shark get octopus to eat.
It's quite a sight, those jaws in a frilly frock.

But I feel no warmth, unless it comes to pass
he ascends from my shark-fin soup, all steam and heat.
Stroke him – you might as well stroke broken glass.

Electrophorus Electricus

The serpent who guards my Eden in the Zoo,
after the monkeys, the monkeys and the bear,
and the emerald fish in their twilight atmosphere,
is the electric eel, who turns on lights for you.

We have grown, myself and that smooth gentleman,
but I am free and he, as round he glides,
has hardly room and brushes all the sides,
though to and fro still goes his crinkly fin.

The small red lamps he lights and his tick, tick, tock,
show he's busy giving his electric shop a shine,
or is a blind man crossing over with a stick.

Better, perhaps, then if you learn in time
that red light functions as a warning sign,
so what comes after Eden's less a shock.

Baby Sea-Horses

They're rather slow at being born quite right.
Their outlines are complete but then the sea
still flows through their insides, they float there free,
their tails have yet to learn to anchor tight.

They want to turn the tide but it's a strain.
Grown out of father's belly-sack, they try.
Two, tail-to-tail, shoot upwards to the sky
but flummox it and have to start again.

To let them practise galloping undisturbed,
they're put in a basin, where beneath the eye
of father, they can have another try.

In that heavy gear his every movement's curbed,
but with his mini-mini-horsepower he'll defend
his offspring, a brave Don Quixote to the end.

Axolotl

He's the ultimate challenge to those poets who
would demonstrate their handiness with rhyme,
yet in Dutch can't find a rhyme for autumn-time.
(He's an amphibian these lines are devoted to.)

They come in black and white but everyone
who sees the two together's bound to choose
the white one. Round his neck a feathery rose
makes it seem a living autopsy's begun.

He fights the black one, eyes a bluish glow,
fiercely contesting a minute scrap of meat –
a clown, with combinations all in white

and tail and gills he's unlikely to outgrow,
he is the frog that's plagued with vertigo,
this amniotic fluid his lifetime fate.

Turtles

Their naked necks project out of the water,
these senior citizens in their Turkish bath.
One clambers up onto a water-lily leaf,
slips down again and puts it off till later.

It's all so still – just aged heads, no more.
No brainwork in each shrivelled, plumpish bud.
Their bodies slumped in waterish brown mud,
discs, with little feet split here and there.

To long for nowt's the art it would appear.
To search, unseen, for equilibrium.
Would worry, hunger, desire then disappear?

Mind rudderless as a little paper-boat,
yet seeming to have found Elysium.
Not Buddhas – muffins, complete with legs, afloat.

Capybara

Brown as an autumn day late in the year,
planted, with feet submerged, on the riverside,
snout of a rabbit, stoic, mascara-eyed,
he stands, a giant rodent, streamlined hair.

The rabbit who, in Carroll's Wonderland,
scurrying to tea, still searching for his fan,
ate the cakes with 'Eat me' printed on,
which made him grow so big, become so grand?

He himself's no longer edible,
no longer food for lion or crocodile.
He's an inflated guinea pig, now Jungle God.

You wouldn't touch him with a six-foot rod.
But size has failed to change him – now he's big
he's still as boring as a guinea-pig.

Otters

Eight otters, lithe as eels, spin round and run,
leaping like mad, yet landing aristocratly.
What one does, so can the other – more acrobatly –
with a single aim in view: now let's have fun.

Never for a moment still, all at a lick,
feeling at everything with busy, busy hands,
scratching, yawning, showing their sharp little fangs,
and always at stepped-up tempo, double-quick.

An otter bite or tastes his fellow-beasts,
as a challenge, as a test, for food, for play.
Then scrambling and tumbling, into their cave they go.

Never a care in the world, for otters know:
life's a permanent party, a thousand feasts,
and depressions come from far, far, far away.

Varan Lizard

When sunning himself run over by a tank?
Or did something go radically wrong when they pumped
    him up?
Rolled smooth by a sizzling iron when a lizard pup?
No room for brains in a skull as thin as a plank.

Reptilian blood is slow and very cold.
He's looking for a tree-trunk near the pane,
where his sensitive fingers can tap out a refrain,
make music out of wood that's turned to mould.

His tuning fork is blue and worn quite flat.
It strikes the note for a chicken's cheepy yell
and vibrates to the death-cry of a mouse or rat.

Oh reader, use your brains and they will tell
you no animal hears things with its tongue and that
is because the varan's tongue is used to smell.

Night Creatures

The bats see life wrapped up from upside down,
their tattered jackets tucked around them tight.
One shakes his cape, then draws himself upright
to act Christopher Lee in ghastly gown.

The sloth plays Captain Hook in fur disguise,
his slender loris now grown quite obese.
She contemplates me with a worried face –
a girl with too much eye-black round her eyes.

They live their night while I sit in the sun
and dream on a terrace close to where they hide
in eternal silence – time not yet begun.

Yet who would choose the black face of the blind?
The theatre of night, life's darkling side?
And who am I to choose – day-tripper kind?

Snow Hare

He's busy changing from brown to white, this hare.
Like a Dürer aquarelle that's turned out wet,
he presents a quaintly speckled silhouette,
a magician's trick repeated every year.

In this fading season, when all that's green grows dun,
his sunburn's changing now to winter-pale.
Already like a white pompon, his tail,
seems in plaster before the winter sports have come.

December 20, the frost's become severe.
A whiter-than-white hare now, proud of ear,
squats in the grass, peers at the snow on high.

He's conjured again out of a black top hat,
but the loss of pigment's not yet quite complete:
on his forehead there's still a spot – his summer eye.

Rattlesnake

Evil rolled up, a measuring-tape for sin,
lies innocently asleep, coiled on the ground.
Scraps of his cast-off coat lie scattered round –
all those who laze in the sun must lose their skin.

A carnivore, he recommended fruit,
but Eve was too slow to grasp his homily.
He rattled away so uneconomically,
flashing his meat-fork wildly in and out.

Paradise, after this, was soon closed down,
the tree was felled, the serpent never seen.
His venom, for spraying apples, won renown.

The symbolic point of this I fear I missed.
I worked in a zoo and there, sweet seventeen,
down by the snake-pit was, for the first time, kissssssed.

Tortoise

He shuffles closer by on leather feet,
his wrinkled head projecting from the shell
he has to lug around with him as well,
his scaly knees bent low beneath its weight.

He can act the Atlas saga with that girth,
despite his lukewarm, slow reptilian state.
Or is that too much? Do I exaggerate?
After all, it's only half a globe, his earth.

His burden's ballast, a protective, stony hide,
a sort of ack-ack fire, solidified:
self-defence has made him heavier than a log.

If only he could wrest his body free,
escape for good the force of gravity,
he could be as light and carefree as a frog.

Day-Trippers

The truly adapted members of the nation,
the day-tripper tribe who do as others do,
are out to test my powers of toleration:
today the trip includes, of course, the zoo.

In training-gear like violent neon-lighting,
(no animals here could equal such display)
with kids for ever bawling, screaming, fighting,
in T-shirts shouting: 'Shit!' 'Drop dead!' 'No way!'

The creatures they have come to stare at here
are imprisoned at our doing – ours the blame,
evolution's two-legged heroes that we are.

To get away from here is all my aim.
I search in vain to get a breath of air,
I look around me, hang my head in shame.